Chinese Love Lyrics

WITH DECORATIVE CUT-OUTS
BY PAUL McPHARLIN

THE PETER PAUPER PRESS
MOUNT VERNON, NEW YORK

Chinese Love Lyrics

FROM MOST ANCIENT

TO MODERN

TIMES

Chinese Love Lyrics

Spring

ANONYMOUS (1005 A.D.)

If I were a tree or a plant

I would feel the soft influence of spring.

Since I am a man . . .

Do not be astonished at my joy.

GERTRUDE L. JOERISSEN

The Vanished Cloud

Nalan Hsin-teh

The bright moon, full of love,
Ought to laugh at me . . .
Laugh at my present plight.
I failed miserably to respond
To the heart of spring,
And now I am wandering all alone and
Whimpering to myself.

Of late, to shun the memories
Of the past, I have sought solace
In friendships everywhere. . . .
But when the moon is pale
And the lamp is burnt to its socket,
In my dream I still try to trace
The vanished cloud.

TERESA LI

The Boat Is Unsteady

THE BOOK OF SONGS

Unsteady is that cypress boat
In the middle of the river.
His two locks looped over his brow,
He swore that truly he was
My comrade, until death would love
   no other.
Oh, mother, ah, Heaven,
That a man could be so false!

Unsteady is that boat of cypress-wood
By that river's side.
His two locks looped over his brow,
He swore that truly he was my mate,
And till death would not fail me.
Oh, mother, ah, Heaven,
That a man could be so false!

ARTHUR WALEY

The Separation

MA HUANG-CHUNG

Daylight! And I must leave.

Belovèd friend, do not rise!

Give me the little lamp

That I may look at thee again,

That I may put all of thee into my heart

And into my soul. . . .

Now, thy lips! I hear the gong

Of the night watchman sounding.

Work leads to evening, and

Each evening brings me to

Thy arms, which are my recompense.

Look! The leaves are covered with pearls

Of dew. . . . A blackbird is whistling.

Until this evening, adieu!

GERTRUDE L. JOERISSEN

It Seems Like Years

THE BOOK OF SONGS

Oh, he is plucking cloth-creeper . . .
For a single day I have not seen him . . .
It seems like three months!

Oh, he is plucking southernwood . . .
For a single day I have not seen him . . .
It seems like three autumns!

Oh, he is plucking mugwort . . .
For a single day I have not seen him . . .
It seems like three years!

ARTHUR WALEY

Watching the Moon

CHIANG CHE-KIN

My belovèd knows
That I watch thee, O moon,
And when thy beams caress her,
Our separation is less cruel.

GERTRUDE L. JOERISSEN

All Because of You

THE BOOK OF SONGS

That mad boy will not speak with me. . . .
Yes, all because of you
I leave my rice untouched.

That mad boy will not eat with me. . . .
Yes, it is all because of you
That I cannot take my rest.

ARTHUR WALEY

A Spring Dream

TSIN TSAN

While I slept, one night,

A spring breeze entered my chamber,

And my spirit floated with it, far, far away

To the borders of the river Kiang, into the

Presence of a young girl

Whose smile, one evening, had made me reel

Like a drunken man.

Brief was my dream.

When I went to sleep the moon was

Just level with the top of the almond tree.

When I woke up, it had not

Moved. One instant was enough

For me to cover the hundred leagues which

Separate me from the Kiang-nan, and

From a young girl with a dangerous smile.

GERTRUDE L. JOERISSEN

Bestowed in Farewell

Tu Mu

She is slender and elegant and not yet
Fourteen, beautiful as the tips of the
Cardamom buds in early spring.
Although the spring wind may blow the
Whole length of the Road of Courtesans,
When they roll up their beaded blinds
There is none to be compared with her.

She has so much passion . . .
Yet tonight it would seem as if she had none.
Although we are drinking for the last time
She fails to force a smile.
But the wax candles seem to understand
And sorrow at our parting; they play
Our parts for us and they weep
Till early dawn.

SOAME JENYNS

The Breath of Spring

ANONYMOUS

The breath of spring is everywhere,
  in every face.
The mimosa casts its delicate shadows . . .
My dreams are butterflies . . .
The fragrance of the quince intoxicates
  like wine.

But I pluck the willow of sorrow.
A gulf divides us, and there is no
  fairy bridge
Of birds to carry me across.

I weep alone before my silver lamp and

Grow frail as Hsiao Man the slender

   beauty.

When shall we share a night like this,

A spring night like this, and meet

   together

Under the full moon?

PETER RUDOLPH

Like the Moon

THE DANCING GIRL WU-HAO

Like the moon in the blue heavens

I am alone in my room.

I have put out the light and

I am weeping.

I weep because you are so far

Away, and because you will never know

How much I love you.

GERTRUDE L. JOERISSEN

14

Going Rowing

Tu Fu

In order to go rowing in our boat
We have waited for the setting of the sun.
A slight breeze ripples the blue surface
And stirs the water lilies.
Along the banks, where the cherry
Blossoms fall like rain,
We catch a glimpse of strolling lovers.

My courteous friends prepare cooling drinks.
The beautiful young girls breathe the perfume
Of the white glycine.

I watch a cloud sailing over us.
Soon, the rain ...
And I shall compose some verses on
The inconstancy of happiness.

GERTRUDE L. JOERISSEN

15

In the Palace of Chao Yang

Li Po

The blossoms have replaced
The snow which made heavy the branches
Of the apricot tree. The breath of early spring
Warms the land, and the branches of
The willow tree tremble with happiness.
The song of the *yang* bird
Awakens the forest. The returning swallows
Fly about the roof.

In the blue palace whirl the dancing girls,
Crowned with wreaths of white glycine.

The fête will last until the moment when
The first light of dawn dances
On the silken curtains.

Now the moon lights up the garden
Strewn with peach blossoms. Come with me,
Pretty maiden! We will go and listen to the
Sound of wings which the bamboos make
In the breeze. . . .

GERTRUDE L. JOERISSEN

By the Willows

THE BOOK OF SONGS

By the willows of the Eastern Gate, whose
Leaves are so thick, at dusk we were to meet;
And now the morning star is bright.

By the willows of the Eastern Gate, whose
Leaves are so close, at dusk we were to meet;
And now the morning star is pale.

ARTHUR WALEY

Birds Singing at Dusk

Li Po

The cool wind of evening
Blows bird-song to the window
Where a maiden sits.
She is embroidering bright flowers
On a piece of silk.

Her head is raised;
Her work falls through her fingers;
Her thoughts have flown to him
Who is away.

"A bird can easily find its mate
Among the leaves,
But all a maiden's tears,
Falling like rain from Heaven,
Will not bring back
Her distant lover."

She bends again to her embroidery:

"I will weave a little verse

Among these flowers of his robe . . .

Perhaps he will read it

And come back again."

PETER RUDOLPH

A River of Love

LI CHIH-YI

I live at the upper end of the River,

And at the lower end live you;

Every day I long to see you but cannot . . .

Though from the same River we drink.

When will the River go dry?

When can my sorrow come to an end?

Only may your heart be like mine . . .

My love for you will not be in vain.

CH'U TA KAO

The Willow Leaf

WAN TSI

A leaf has just fallen from the willow tree. . . .
It is floating now upon the water.

In my heart, also, time has done its work.
I am separated from the young woman
Whom I loved too much . . .
And I wait, in peace, my destiny.

I watch the leaf from the willow tree. . . . Ah!
The eddying current carries it back
Toward the branch from which it has fallen. . . .

GERTRUDE L. JOERISSEN

The Call

TS'UI CHUO-FU

I watched the glittering rings of
A young woman who was seated on

20

The terrace of the Birds of Bronze.

She was brushing her eyebrows, and

Her red dress flamed in the sun.

A messenger came to tell her that

The king was waiting for her. . . .

She perfumed her arms and her knees,

And rose to her feet. . . .

GERTRUDE L. JOERISSEN

The Message from Afar

ANONYMOUS

Deep green lies the grass
Along the river. Far away
The road stretches, a road without end. . . .
I dare not think of the
Endlessness of that road.

Last night I saw him in a dream. . . .
In a dream I had him here beside me.
Suddenly I awoke to feel again his absence. . . .
Far, far away is he in unknown lands.
I turn away, not daring to see
His empty place.

The withered mulberry knows the cruelty
Of Heaven's wind. Ocean knows
The bitterness of Heaven's cold.
Others are happy in the loves

Of their homes. No one is there
To talk with me.

From a far place there has come a guest.
He has brought me the present of
A pair of carp. I order the little boy
To prepare them; and in one of them ...
He finds a strip of paper.
Kneeling down I read it.
The first line says: "Cherish thyself for me."
The second line says: "Think of me always."

ALAN SIMMS LEE

Here by the Wall-Gate

THE BOOK OF SONGS

Oh, you with the blue collar,
On and on I think of you.
Even though I do not go to you ...
You might surely send me news?

23

Oh, you with the blue collar,

Always and ever I long for you.

Even though I do not go to you . . .

You might surely sometimes come?

Here by the wall-gate I pace

To and fro. One day when I do not see you

Is like three months.

ARTHUR WALEY

Love, What a Source of Sorrows

Wu Yung

Lingering, lingering, pulsating . . .

Pulsating, two hearts beat as one.

Fine as gossamer, vast as the waves,

Inconstant as the moon, frail as

A flower, this strange thing that we

  call love . . .

What a prolific source of sorrow it is!

TERESA LI

On the Banks of Jo-Yeh

Li Po

On the banks of Jo-Yeh, some young girls
Are gathering water lilies.
They call to each other and laughingly
Hide themselves among the bamboos.
Their lovely dresses which perfume
    the breeze
Are reflected in the water.

25

Between the willows on the bank
Some horsemen pass — one horse neighs.
His master looks about in vain on all sides,
Then goes his way.

One of the young girls drops her water lilies
And clasps her fast beating heart.

GERTRUDE L. JOERISSEN

Among the Bamboos

Tu Fu

Bring me no more flowers. Bring me
Cypress branches in which to plunge my face.

When the sun has disappeared behind
The mountains I put on my robe of blue
With the thin sleeves and go and sleep
Among the bamboos which she loved.

GERTRUDE L. JOERISSEN

When a Beggar Beholds You...

ANONYMOUS (c. 324 A.D.)

When the breeze inflates
Your two robes of silk, you look like a
Goddess enveloped in clouds.

When you pass, the flowers
Of the mulberry tree drink in
Your perfume. When you carry the lilacs
That you have gathered, they
Tremble with joy.

Bands of gold encircle your ankles,
Stones of blue gleam in your girdle . . .
A bird of jade has made its nest in your hair.
The roses of your cheeks mirror themselves in
The great pearls of your collar.

When you look at me
I see the river Yuen flowing. . . .

27

When you speak to me

I hear the music of the wind among

   the pines

Of my own country.

When a horseman meets you at dusk

He thinks it is already dawn, and brutally

He brings his horse to a standstill.

...When a beggar beholds you,

He forgets his hunger.

GERTRUDE L. JOERISSEN

The Trees of Jade

Li Po

It snowed, that night, in the garden

Of Liang. I was cold and

You were quite unconscious of it.

Tonight, I watched the trees of jade

28

Under which, in days gone by, I used

To wait for you.   GERTRUDE L. JOERISSEN

That Promise Which You Made Me

THE EMPEROR HI TSONG

And that promise which you made me
Last night under the flowering acacia tree?

... But where is the dew which made
Its blossoms heavy?   GERTRUDE L. JOERISSEN

29

Thinking of a Friend

YANG KI

It is going to rain....
The wind bruises the flowers of my jasmine
And whirls away the petals of the peonies,
Scattering them over the ground.
It lifts the blinds at the windows.
It ruffles the young girls' hair.

I am sad. I think of my friend.
The blue sky, the green sea, and the
White mountains separate us.
Ah, if those birds could carry to my friend
The letters which I write to her!
If this little stream could carry to her
The petals from my peonies!

The magnolias gleam in the shadows . . .
But I cannot touch my lute.

I watch the moon, which is like a

Great magnolia blossom.

I will not sing. I will not play.

I want to give myself entirely to my sadness.

GERTRUDE L. JOERISSEN

The Empty Room

Li Po

When the beautiful woman lived in this

    room

It was filled with many flowers.

She has gone, the beautiful woman, and

Her couch awaits her no more.

Three years she has been gone, but

Her perfume lingers still.

Three years!... From grief, the

Leaves are falling!

GERTRUDE L. JOERISSEN

The First Full-moon Night

Ou-yang Hsiu

Last year, in the First Full-moon Night,
At the Flower Market, lanterns were
As bright as day; when the moon
Came up on the top of the willows,
My love and I met after dusk.

This year, in the First Full-moon Night,
The moon and lanterns are the same as
   before.

But I do not see the one who

Was with me last year, and tears wet the

Sleeves of my spring gown.

CH'U TA KAO

The Winter of Love

CHANG WU-CHIEN

The red tulip which I gave you . . .

You let fall into the dust. I picked it up.

It was all white.

In that little moment the snow

Fell upon our love.

GERTRUDE L. JOERISSEN

Fading in the Springtime

WENG T'ING CHUN

The careful knot of hair
Lies low
Upon her neck; her long and narrow
Eyebrows are painted skilfully.

Yet, following you, her thoughts
Are wandering afar...
In this season of a hundred flowers,
She grows thin and pale.

PETER RUDOLPH

Off in a Boat

THE BOOK OF SONGS

The two of you went off in a boat,
Floating... floating far away.
Longingly I think of you;
My heart within is sore.

34

The two of you went off in a boat,

Floating . . . floating you sped away.

Longingly I think of you.

Oh may you come to no harm!

ARTHUR WALEY

The Dream at Midnight

WEI CHUANG

Dreaming at midnight,

Last night I met you and we spoke again.

As of old, your cheeks were blossoms,

Your eyes were often lowered,

Your eyebrows were spring willow-leaves.

You were half gay and half demure . . .

Thinking you should go away . . .

Lingering still.

Then I awakened, and wept

That it was a dream.

PETER RUDOLPH

35

There Is a Man So Fair

THE BOOK OF SONGS

By that swamp's shore grow reeds
And lotus. There is a man so fair . . .
Oh, how can I cure my wound?
Day and night I can do nothing;
As a flood my tears flow.

By that swamp's shore grow reeds
And lotus-flowers. There is a man so fair . . .

Well-made, big and stern. Day and night

I can do nothing . . .

Face on pillow I toss and turn.

ARTHUR WALEY

Tip-Toeing to Her Lover

PRINCE LI YU

The flowers bright, the moon dim,

And a light mist eddying about . . .

Tonight is meant for me to go to my love.

Off with my stockings;

I walk down the fragrant steps . . .

With my gold-lined slippers in hand.

At the south side of the Painted Hall

We meet; I fall trembling in his arms and say:

"Because it was so hard to come to you,

Let me have your very best caress."

CH'U TA KAO

A Pair of Plantain Trees

PRINCE LI CHIN

A tress of cloud! A shuttle of jade!
A pale, pale robe of thin, thin gauze!
A nameless grace playing about
Her knitted brows like a faint shade!

Autumn gales start, echoed by the rain.
Outside the window screen a pair of
Plantain trees grow wide apart. The long,
Long night wears out a longing heart.

TERESA LI

Come, Yoke the Horses

THE BOOK OF SONGS

How it tapered, the bamboo rod
With which you fished in the Ch'i!
It is not that I do not love you,
But it is so far that I cannot come.

The Well Spring is on the left;
The Ch'i river on the right.
When a girl is married she is far
From brothers, from father and mother.

The Ch'i river is on the right,
The Well Spring is on the left;
But, oh, the grace of his loving smile!
Oh, the quiver of his girdle stones!

The Ch'i spreads its waves;
Oars of juniper, boat of pine-wood.
Come, yoke the horses, let us drive away,
That I may be rid at last of my pain.

ARTHUR WALEY

The Curtain of Pearls

WANG CHANG-LING

Her lute in her hand,
She carelessly pushed aside the curtain

39

Of pearls, so that the breath of spring
Might flow into her room;
But she saw the moon, and it was
Sorrow that entered in.

Her face hidden in her folded arms
She remembers a garden, all blue
In the moonlight, where once she listened
To words of love.

GERTRUDE L. JOERISSEN

Yet She Lingers

THE BOOK OF SONGS

Cold blows the northern wind,
Thick falls the snow. Be kind to me,
   love me,
Take my hand and go with me.
Yet she lingers, yet she wavers.
There is no time to lose.

The north wind whistles, whirls
The falling snow. Be kind to me,
   love me,
Take my hand and go home with me.
Yet she lingers, yet she wavers!
There is no time to lose.

Nothing is redder than the fox, nothing
Blacker than the crow. Be kind to me,
   love me,
Take my hand and ride with me.
Yet she lingers, yet she wavers!
There is no time to lose.

ARTHUR WALEY

Sun in the East

THE BOOK OF SONGS

Sun in the east!

This lovely man is in my house,

Is in my home, his foot is

Upon my doorstep.

Moon in the east!

This lovely man is in my bower,

Is in my bower. His foot is

Upon my threshold.

ARTHUR WALEY

Not Just As Requital

THE BOOK OF SONGS

She threw a quince to me . . .

In requital I gave her a bright girdle-gem.

No, not just as requital . . .

But meaning I would love her for ever.

42

She threw a tree-peach to me . . .

As requital I gave her a bright green-stone.

No, not just as requital . . .

But meaning I would love her for ever.

She threw a tree-plum to me . . .

In requital I gave her a bright jet-stone.

No, not just as requital . . .

But meaning I would love her for ever.

ARTHUR WALEY

The Maidens Gathering Lilies

Li Po

At Yé-Ki, young girls gathering

Water lilies sing as they row. If a stranger

Looks at them they hide themselves

Behind their bunches of water lilies

And pretend to be confused . . .

And they laugh, and laugh.

GERTRUDE L. JOERISSEN

The Garden of Golden Valley

Tu Mu

The splendid glories of the past
Have been pulverized into fragrant dust.
The stream flows on indifferently, and
The grass keeps spring to itself.

At sunset, the singing birds lament the
Passing away of the east wind. The falling

Flowers recall the pretty one who

Threw herself from a high balcony.

TERESA LI

The Song of Love

CHEN TEUO-TSAN

Thy hands are two flowers of *lân*.

Thy feet are two buds of magnolia blossoms.

Thy cheeks are two tulips.

Thy mouth is a drop of coral.

Thy breasts are two oranges of Chiang-nân.

Thy perfume is that of spring.

Thy voice is more seductive than the

Song of the breeze among the willows when

They are turning green. Thy breath is

More intoxicating than the odor of a

   pagoda

Where the incense burns.

Thou art more beautiful

Than an apricot blossom bathed in the

   moonlight.

Thou art all the flowers, all the perfumes;

Thou art all the splendors of the world.

When I think of thee

I no longer envy the Gods.

GERTRUDE L. JOERISSEN

Thoughts in a Temple

NALAN HSIN-TEH

The fire in my heart is turned to ashes....

I feel like a monk; only

My head is still unshaven.

O poor heart! How the wind and rain

Have worn you out! How the

Partings from friends, dead and alive,

Have torn you to pieces!

This orphan-like candlestick
Appears like an old friend to me.

There remains one thing alone that keeps me
From a complete Awakening . . .
Love still smoulders in the ashes of my heart!

TERESA LI

For Her Birthday

FENG YEN-CHI

A feast being spread in spring-time,
With a cup of green wine and a
Joyous song, I repeat my salutation and
Offer my three wishes:
First, may you have a long life; second,
May I have good health; third, may we live
As the swallows on the beam,
Happily together all the year round.

CH'U TA KAO

Speak While There Is Time

THE BOOK OF SONGS

Plop fall the plums; but there are still seven.
Let those gentlemen that would court me
Come while it is lucky!

Plop fall the plums; there are still three.
Let any gentleman that would court me
Come before it is too late!

Plop fall the plums; in shallow baskets
We lay them. Any gentleman who would
Court me had better speak while there is time.

ARTHUR WALEY

Two Swallows

Li Po

Two swallows, and two swallows . . .
Always, the swallows fly in couples. When
They see a tower of jade, or a
    lacquered pavilion,
One never perches there without the other.
When they find a balustrade of marble
Or a gilded window, they never separate.

Once there were two swallows. . . .
When the girder of cedar which sheltered
Their nest took fire, the two birds sought
Refuge in a palace of the king of Wu, but
The palace of the king of Wu burned down
And the male and the little ones
Burned too. When she returned,
The female sat contemplating the ruins.

This story saddens me infinitely.

GERTRUDE L. JOERISSEN

The Crushed Peony

ANONYMOUS

A peony blossom
Bepearled with dew-drops she plucked
And, coming smiling across the courtyard,
Asked her love: "Whose beauty excels,
The flower's or mine?"

In order to tease her, he gave
All his praise to the flower; she
In a moment of girlish anger, crumpled
The blossom and threw it over him.

CH'U TA KAO

The South Country

WEI CHUANG

Thus all the world
Praises the South Country to me:

"It best befits you, a wanderer,
There to spend your life.
The waters in spring look bluer than
   the skies,
And rains will lull you to sleep
In the painted boat.

"The wine-shop maids there
Are as charming as the moon,
Their glowing arms like frozen frost
And drifted snow. Do not go home
Before you are old, lest you should
Break your heart."

Now I recall the joys
Of the South Country: when I was young
And my spring attire was light,
On horseback I roamed by the arched
   bridge,
And on the terraces red sleeves

Beckoned at me; behind the emerald
    screen
And the gold-knockered doors I was
    drunken
And slept amid the thick-growing flowers
Of love. Were I to see those flowers
Once again, even though my hair grew
    white,
I swear I would never come home.

CH'U TA KAO

My Lord Summons Me

THE BOOK OF SONGS

My lord is all aglow.
In his left hand he holds the reed-pipe,
With his right he summons me
To make free with him.
Oh, the joy!

My lord is care-free.

In his left hand he holds the dancing plumes,

With his right he summons me

To sport with him.

Oh, the joy!

ARTHUR WALEY

The Peach Trees Were Flowering

NALAN HSIN TEH

The weather is getting cold. . . .

The wine lies like poison on my heart. . . .

On the window beats the rain.

The fading fragrance, like a little pupil,

Is simulating the feeling of autumn.

"Cheer up, cheer up!" I say to my heart,

But tears have stolen into my blue gown.

Yearnings for my love keep me

Sober in defiance of the wine. . . .

I lie listlessly in my lonely bed. . . .

I remember that when I parted from her,

The peach-trees were flowering, and the

Willows waving their tender locks.

TERESA LI

The Outrage

MA HUANG-CHUNG

One moonlit night I hung

Upon her door a garland of apple blossoms,

then

I made my flute send forth a song of love.

The next day I met her. Some red carnations

That grow in the garden of my neighbor
Adorned her hair.

I shut myself up in my room;
I broke my lute; and I wept for long.

GERTRUDE L. JOERISSEN

To Whom Can I Tell

ANONYMOUS

How brilliant is the moon
Shining upon my silk-curtained bed!
Sorrow denies me sleep. Throwing a robe
About me, I pace to and fro.
Though my distant Lord says he is happy,
I would that he came swiftly.
Lonely I go out and my heart is
Perplexed. To whom can I tell
My bitter thoughts? I return to my room;
And my robe is wet with tears.

ALAN SIMMS LEE

Inscription on a Tomb

ANONYMOUS (1015 A.D.)

Prostrate before the Buddhist Virgin,
So merciful to the unhappy,
I do not ask her that I may be born again or
That I may be kept in Paradise.
But I ask her to let fall upon my head
One of the dewdrops that tremble on the
End of her wand of willow, in order
That I may become a lotus flower,
    which he,
Perhaps, some day will pluck.

GERTRUDE L. JOERISSEN

The Thunder Growls

THE BOOK OF SONGS

Wild and windy was the day;
You looked at me and laughed, but

The jest was cruel, and the laughter mocking.
My heart within is sore.

There was a great sandstorm that day;
Kindly you made as though to come,
Yet neither came nor went away.
Long, long my thoughts.

A great wind and darkness;
Day after day it is dark. I lie awake,
I cannot sleep, and gasp with longing.

ARTHUR WALEY

Then I Gave Thanks

CHANG WU-CHIEN

I cursed the rain for
Pounding upon my roof and driving
    away sleep.
I cursed the wind
For ravaging my garden.

Then you entered; and I gave thanks
To the rain because you must put off ·
Your wet dress; and I gave thanks to
    the wind
That he came and blew out my lamp.

ALAN SIMMS LEE

The Lost Flute

CHANG WU-CHIEN

In long black lines the wild geese
Cross the sky. In the trees

One sees the deserted nests. . . .
Winter heaviness seems to have
Settled upon the mountains.

Close to my fountain I found your
Flute of jade which you lost last summer.
The tall grass had screened it from
Our searching. But now the grass is dead and
The flute lay glistening in the sun.

I have been thinking of our love which has lain
So long buried under our scruples.

GERTRUDE L. JOERISSEN

The Peach Blossom

TSE TSI

I gathered a rosy flower from
A peach tree and offered it to my belovèd,
Whose mouth is as tiny and as pink
As a peach blossom.

I took from its nest a

Black-winged swallow, and offered it to

My belovèd, whose eyebrows are like

The wings of a swallow.

The next day the peach blossom

Had faded, and the swallow had flown away

Through the window looking out

Over the Blue Mountains.

But the lips of my belovèd are always rosy,

And her black eyebrows

Have not flown away.

GERTRUDE L. JOERISSEN

The Fisherman

Li Po

The earth has swallowed the snow.

Again we see the plum-trees in blossom.

The new willow-leaves are gold,
The waters of the lake are silver.

Now the butterflies powdered with gold
Lay velvet heads within the hearts of flowers.

In his still boat
The fisherman pulls up his dripping net,
Rippling the still water.

He thinks of a girl at home,
Like a dark swallow in the nest.
He thinks of a girl at home . . .
Waiting like a swallow for her mate.

PETER RUDOLPH

The Jewel

WAN TSI

On my flute of ebony
I played to you the most impassioned
Songs that I know, but your eyes
Followed the flight of pigeons and
You would not listen.

I gave you a poem in which
I praised your beauty, but you tore it up ...
Throwing the pieces on the waters of the lake,
Because, as you said, there were
No lotus petals there.

I would have given you a wondrous jewel,
Limpid and cold as a Winter's night, but
I keep it because it is like your heart.

ALAN SIMMS LEE